IN THE NEWS Need to Know

Climate Migrants

by Ashley Kuehl

Consultant: Caitlin Krieck, Social Studies Teacher and Instructional Coach, The Lab School of Washington

Minneapolis, Minnesota

Credits

Cover and title page, © Cathy Withers-Clarke/Adobe Stock and © LIGHTFIELD STUDIOS/Adobe Stock and © poco_bw/Adobe Stock and © Riccardo Niels Mayer/Adobe Stock and © Melinda Nagy/Adobe Stock; 5, © Levente Bodo/Adobe Stock; 7, © sakurra/Adobe Stock; 9, © David McNew/Getty Images; 11, © Aerial Archives/Alamy Stock Photo; 13, © Ed Ram/Getty Images; 15, © Bilanol/Getty Images; 17, © Joe Raedle/Getty Images; 19, © Peter Treanor/Alamy Stock Photo; 21, © FG Trade/Getty Images; 23, © Arni/UN Archives; 25, © Miroslav Hlavko/Shutterstock; 27, © Roy Perring/Alamy Stock Photo; 28TL, © Bloomberg/Getty Images; 28ML, © Public Domain/Wikimedia; 28BL, © World Resources Institute Staff/Wikimedia

Bearport Publishing Company Product Development Team

Publisher: Jen Jenson; Director of Product Development: Spencer Brinker; Managing Editor: Allison Juda; Editor: Cole Nelson; Associate Editor: Naomi Reich; Associate Editor: Tiana Tran; Art Director: Colin O'Dea; Designer: Kim Jones; Designer: Kayla Eggert; Product Development Specialist: Owen Hamlin

Statement on Usage of Generative Artificial Intelligence

Bearport Publishing remains committed to publishing high-quality nonfiction books. Therefore, we restrict the use of generative AI to ensure accuracy of all text and visual components pertaining to a book's subject. See BearportPublishing.com for details.

Quote Sources

Page 28: Greta Thunberg from "Thunberg, UN urge quick action on climate migration," *The Hill*, January 27, 2023; Carlos Del Toro from "SECNAV Delivers Remarks at the University of the Bahamas," *Navy.mil*, March 1, 2023; Al Gore from "'We can reclaim control of our destiny,' Al Gore says of climate change," *Politico*, December 24, 2023.

Library of Congress Cataloging-in-Publication Data is available at www.loc.gov or upon request from the publisher.

ISBN: 979-8-89232-762-6 (hardcover)
ISBN: 979-8-89232-939-2 (paperback)
ISBN: 979-8-89232-849-4 (ebook)

Copyright © 2025 Bearport Publishing Company. All rights reserved. No part of this publication may be reproduced in whole or in part, stored in any retrieval system, or transmitted in any form or by any means, electronic, mechanical, photocopying, recording, or otherwise, without written permission from the publisher.

For more information, write to Bearport Publishing, 5357 Penn Avenue South, Minneapolis, MN 55419.

Contents

Shrinking Islands 4
A Change in Climate 6
Forced to Move 10
Drying Out. 12
Stronger Storms 14
Returning Home. 16
A Difficult Trip 18
Resources for All 20
Protecting Migrants 22
What Happens Next? 26

Voices in the News 28
SilverTips for Success 29
Glossary 30
Read More 31
Learn More Online 31
Index 32
About the Author 32

Shrinking Islands

More than 500,000 people live in the Maldives. But many in this island nation are in danger. Seas are rising because of **climate** change. The water is covering more land. The Maldives could soon be underwater. People may be forced to leave. They could become climate **migrants**.

> Earth's climate has always changed. But this used to happen slowly. It took thousands of years. The climate has changed faster and faster in recent years.

A Change in Climate

Human actions have sped up climate change. People burn **fossil fuels** for energy. This heats our homes and runs our cars. It gives power to businesses. But burning these fuels puts extra **greenhouse gases** into our **atmosphere**. Those gases trap heat around Earth. This makes Earth warmer.

> Not all energy sources make greenhouse gases. Solar power uses the energy from the sun. Some power plants use the wind. And some are even making power using heat from beneath Earth's crust.

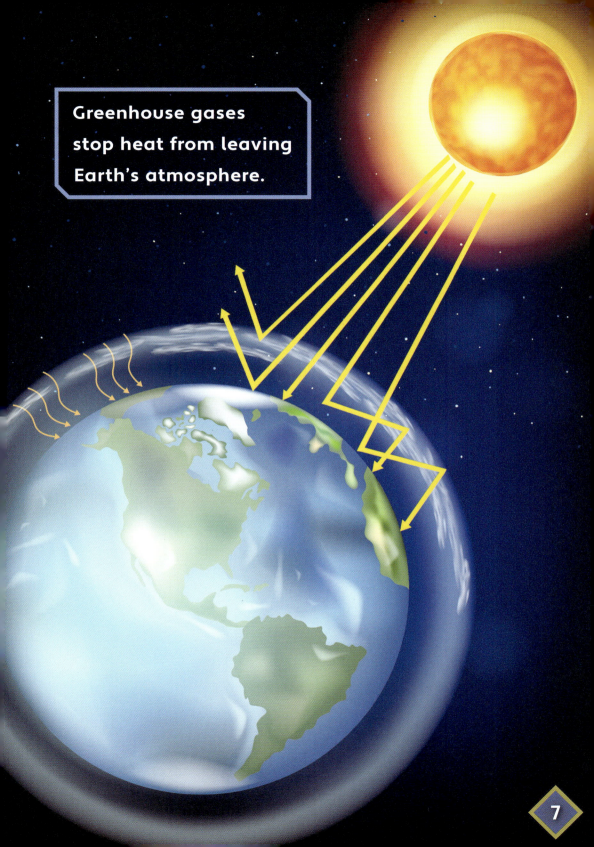

Climate change causes more extreme weather. Damaging storms are more likely. They may lead to floods. Climate change can also cause more **droughts**. Dry weather can make dangerous wildfires more likely. Any of these things can force people to leave their homes.

In 2024, the Park Fire in California impacted more than 20,000 people. It was not safe for them to stay in their homes. About 1,300 firefighters worked together to stop the fire.

Forced to Move

People who leave their homes because of climate change are called climate **migrants**. These people leave for many reasons. They may not have enough food and water anymore. Sometimes, their homes are destroyed in climate disasters.

> Some climate migrants can move to a safer area in their state or country. Others have to make long journeys. They may have to travel to other countries.

Storms may wash away the land homes stand on.

Drying Out

A drought happens when an area gets less rainfall than usual. Droughts can make lakes and rivers smaller or even dry them out. People need water from rivers and lakes for drinking. They use the water for growing **crops**. Many people also fish for food in these rivers and lakes.

> Starting in 2020, Ethiopia and Somalia were hit with a drought that lasted three years. It was the longest in each country's history. Farmers could not grow any food. More than a million people had to leave their homes.

Stronger Storms

Climate change has made hurricanes more extreme. Heavy winds from these storms can damage homes. Some people cover their windows with wood to stop this. But the biggest risk is water coming to shore with the storm. Flood water can destroy houses and businesses.

Hurricanes form in late summer. They need warm ocean waters to get started. As climate change warms Earth, it heats the ocean. This may make more hurricanes each year.

Returning Home

Some climate migrants have to leave for only a short time. If their old homes become safe again, they may move back. But sometimes, whole towns are destroyed by climate disasters. The people who lived in these places cannot go back. They must find new homes.

After bad storms, some people come back and build new homes. But not everyone has money to rebuild. They have to move to find a new place to live.

A Difficult Trip

There are migrants who move to countries with less extreme weather. But many do not have money to travel. These climate migrants have to walk. Traveling across flooded land or escaping wildfires can be dangerous. It can also be hard to get food or shelter along the way.

Some migrants have **disabilities** that make travel difficult. They may not be able to move without help. It can be harder for them to get to a safe place.

Sometimes, climate migrants end up living in tent cities or camps.

Resources for All

Some governments welcome climate migrants. But others stop migrants from crossing their borders. They may not have enough resources for new migrants. It can be hard to get enough food for large numbers of people.

There are countries that are afraid migrants will take away jobs or resources. They make **immigration** hard. This means there are fewer places for climate migrants to find new homes.

Many people join groups to bring food to migrants around the world.

21

Protecting Migrants

International laws protect people who have to leave their homes. But climate migrants aren't included in many of these laws. So, governments and organizations are finding new ways to help. The United Nations has plans to give shelter and clean water to future climate migrants.

In 1951, nearly 150 countries around the world signed an agreement to take in **refugees**. But there weren't climate migrants at this time. They are not included in the agreement.

Many countries are trying to help people before they become climate migrants. Some are collecting clean water for people living through droughts. Others are helping build stronger houses in case of hurricanes. Still others are protecting important lakes and rivers so they don't run out of water.

Using solar or wind energy could help slow climate change. This could protect people from becoming climate migrants.

A wind farm

What Happens Next?

All around the world, people are working together to help climate migrants. Scientists study which places will probably have climate disasters. They work with governments to protect people from a changing planet. This work helps migrants now and in the future.

Seawalls protect homes and businesses from rising water levels. Some seawalls are built to give safe places for plants and animals to live.

This wall in Plymouth, England, helps people and acts as a habitat for ocean life.

Voices in the News

People have many things to say about climate migrants. Some of their voices can be heard in the news.

Greta Thunberg
Climate Activist

"This is a question of life and death for countless people having to flee because of the climate crisis."

Carlos Del Toro
U.S. Navy Secretary

"Climate change is one of the . . . most complex issues we have ever faced."

Al Gore
Former vice president of the United States

"If we don't take action, there could be as many as one billion climate refugees . . . in the next several decades."

SilverTips for SUCCESS

⭐ SilverTips for REVIEW

Review what you've learned. Use the text to help you.

Define key terms

climate change
droughts
fossil fuels

greenhouse gases
migrants

Check for understanding

What are climate migrants?

Why do climate migrants leave their homes?

How is climate change affecting where people live?

Think deeper

What effects of climate change do you see where you live? How does that compare with the experiences of climate migrants?

⭐ SilverTips on TEST-TAKING

- **Make a study plan.** Ask your teacher what the test is going to cover. Then, set aside time to study a little bit every day.

- **Read all the questions carefully.** Be sure you know what is being asked.

- **Skip any questions** you don't know how to answer right away. Mark them and come back later if you have time.

Glossary

atmosphere a layer of gases that surrounds a planet

climate the pattern of weather in a place over a long period of time

crops plants grown for food

disabilities physical or mental conditions that affect a person's ability to do certain tasks

droughts long periods of time with less rain or snow than is typical

fossil fuels natural gas, coal, or oil formed from plant or animal remains

greenhouse gases gases, such as carbon dioxide or methane, that trap warm air in the atmosphere

immigration moving from one country to live in another country

migrants people that move from one place to another

refugees people forced to leave their homelands because of war or other dangers

Read More

Bergin, Raymond. *Terrible Storms (What on Earth?: Climate Change Explained).* Minneapolis: Bearport Publishing, 2022.

Faust, Daniel R. *Global Warming (Climate Change: Need to Know).* Minneapolis: Bearport Publishing, 2024.

Hill, Christina. *Climate Migrants: A Graphic Guide (The Climate Crisis).* Minneapolis: Graphic Universe, 2024.

Learn More Online

1. Go to **FactSurfer.com** or scan the QR code below.
2. Enter "**Climate Migrants**" into the search box.
3. Click on the cover of this book to see a list of websites.

Index

climate change 4, 6–8, 10, 14, 24
drought 8, 12, 24
Ethiopia 12
farmers 12, 26
flooding 8, 14, 16, 18
fossil fuels 6
immigration 20
laws 22
Maldives 4–5
refugees 23
seawalls 26–27
Somalia 12
storms 8, 11, 14
United Nations 22
weather 8, 18
wildfires 8, 18

About the Author

Ashley Kuehl is an editor and writer specializing in nonfiction for young people. She lives in Minneapolis, MN.